DAVID LITTLE

Chinese Kenpo Karate

My Journey Into The Martial Arts – Why I Chose Chinese Kenpo Karate – From Beginner To Instructor

First edition

This book was professionally typeset on Reedsy.
Find out more at reedsy.com

Chinese Kenpo Karate

Dedication

I myself, David Little, would like to dedicate this book to all of my past Instructors and Students I have met along the way in my Journey into the Martial Arts. I have learned something from all of you. With your dedication to the Arts, in the various studies of fighting systems, you have made this book possible.

Contents

Acknowledgement

First of all, I want to thank Chuck Sullivan and Vic LeRoux, the founders of the International Karate Connection Association. When they decided to put their Chinese Kenpo Karate training into a video home study course, it changed my life as well as thousands of other students.

I would also like to thank Gary Emerson, my Brother John Little, and Charlie Page. They accepted the challenge of being my workout partners, while I was progressing through the Chinese Kenpo Training Course.

I want to thank Tim Stewart, for being my Certification Student up to Brown Belt, and Keith Blanchard for being my Certification Student for Black Belt. Without their dedication, I would have never had the opportunity to complete my training for the "IKCA Certified Instructor Title".

Chapter 1

Introduction

This book is about my personal journey throughout my life, while studying various martial arts systems. From being a bullied 8 year old, to presently, a retired Chinese Kenpo Karate Instructor. You will read about it all, when it began, my influences, training in my 20's, 30's, 40's, and 50's. How and why I chose Chinese Kenpo Karate as the Art to teach to others.

2

Chapter 2

My Martial Arts Journey Begins

Childhood Bullies At School

The year was 1967, I was around 8 years old, living in California. My father was in the Air Force, we lived on base. During the summer, my friend and I used to hang out and play at the school playground. I was getting ready to leave and walk home, I was approached by two older boys I didn't know. I knew they were older and bigger than me, a grade ahead of me.

One of them grabbed me from behind and held my arms behind my back. The other proceeded to punch me in the stomach, while the other was holding tight from behind. This was the first time in my life that I remember being bullied. I remember crying and telling them to stop, they just laughed and got on their bikes and rode away. I ran home and told my parents that two bigger boys had beaten me up.

A few days later, my Father took me to a Judo Class that was being held on Base. The first day we observed this small Japanese man throwing a large Man around like he was a rag doll. My father enrolled me into that Judo Class, after talking with the Instructor (that small Japanese man wasn't much taller than me).

My Friend from school also attended the same classes. One day, the instructor put my friend and I in a Judo match together. I think my friend's head butted my nose, by accident. I noticed I was bleeding all over my white Gi and white Judo mats. I didn't stop the match, I wanted to win, and I did win the match.

I continued the Judo classes and earned an Orange Belt. My Father was transferred, so we moved to Oklahoma in 1968. My Father was stationed in Korea for 13 months, my Mother and us kids lived in Oklahoma with my Mother's Parents.

Chapter 3

My Martial Arts Influences

I didn't have the opportunity to continue my Judo training; it wasn't available where I lived in Oklahoma. So I spent time playing junior league baseball. While I was at school in Oklahoma, I got bullied again, I was in the 5th grade.

The only exposure I had to martial arts was from watching Television. I remember watching shows like, Lost in Space, The Green Hornet, and Andy Griffith Show. I knew who Kato was from the Green Hornet, but I didn't know who Bruce Lee was yet. I knew Barnie Fife on Andy Griffith, and his Judo chop, haha.

After my Father came back from Korea, we moved to Minnesota, up on the Canadian border, another Air Base. I got bullied again, I was in 7th grade then, and the bully was in 8th grade.

Well this time, I decided to try some Judo I remembered. When the bully came at me, I grabbed his arm and stuck my leg out and tripped him. He went face down and was embarrassed. I was with my girlfriend at the time it happened, no way he was going to beat me in front of her.

The Day I Was Attacked By A Man

While still living in Minnesota, when I was 12, I was attacked at the playground by an Adult. Here is what happened, I was pushing my little sister on the swing set. This other girl, younger than me, started pushing my sister's swing higher and higher, while I was talking with my girlfriend.

I went over and told the girl to stop, because my sister was crying. The girl ran home and got her Dad, they lived right across from the playground. Next thing I know, while my back was turned, I was grabbed and pummeled by the girl's Father.

I left my bike at the playground and ran home screaming. I got home and told my parents, I was bleeding on my face where I got punched. My Father asked who it was that beat me, I told him the First SGT of the Base, I knew this because the girl told me this, I guess to intimidate me.

My Father went down to talk to the girl's Father, I watched from a distance. I remember my Father told him to never touch any of his kids again, while he pointed his index finger at the First SGT. The next thing that happened, he punched my Father, while my Father was down on the ground, the man sat on my Dad and pummeled him.

I ran home and told my Mother, she called the Air Police. The Police arrested the First SGT, he was a large man, and took 2 men to man handle him. My Father didn't fight back because he had one year to go to retire from the Air Force, and didn't want to screw that up. My Dad walked around for a while, looking like a pummeled boxer, with cuts and bruises on his face.

I think that incident got me interested in martial arts again. I told myself that was never going to happen to me. It was about this time 1972, the Kung Fu Series was on TV. I couldn't wait for the next episode to see what Kaine was going to do next.

We moved from Minnesota to Arizona, this is where my Father retired from the Air Force. After that, we moved back to Oklahoma, where I finished 8th grade and Graduated High School. I didn't have any more incidents of fighting while I was still in school.

Meeting A Black Belt In Basic Training

After graduating High School, I joined the Army. It was here while in Basic Training I met a Black Belt in Karate. He was in our Platoon, I remember watching him go outside when we had free time, and kicking a tree. I asked him what he was doing, he said he was practicing his Karate kicks on the tree. I had never seen this in person, only on Kung Fu the TV series.

That was another positive influence on me. I didn't have any fighting occur while I was in the Army, but I came close a couple times though. I usually talked my way out of fighting, but saw many fights while I was serving in the Army.

Meeting A Black Belt On My Job

When I was discharged from the Army, we moved back to Tulsa. But now, I had a pregnant wife and had to find a job. The wife and I stayed with my parents until we got our own apartment. I had started a job working at a pipeline equipment company. While working there, I found out that a certain guy was a Karate Black Belt, and that he gave classes after work.

I joined the class with another friend from work. My friend ended up with a broken foot, he kicked the board wrong. That was another influence in my journey to learn more about the martial arts. This was in 1981, I was 22 with my first daughter born that year.

Chuck Norris and Bruce Lee

In 1982 I went to work as a Letter Carrier with the Post Office. The wife and I went to the Drive-in Movies one night, there was a double feature. A Chuck Norris movie was first, then after was a Bruce Lee movie. Those two movies had a big influence on me, when I saw Chuck Norris doing all those jumping spinning kicks, I was just amazed. Then when the Bruce Lee movie started, I thought he was the fastest I had ever seen. It was the movie where Bruce Lee and Chuck Norris fight each other in the Roman Coliseum.

Kung Fu Theater

There was a show back in the mid 1980's called Kung Fu theater. You might remember, if you're around my age or older. The words never matched the lips moving, the voices were dubbed in English. They also did a lot of high wire acrobatic moves. This is where I saw Jackie Chan for the first time.

Jhoon Rhee and Jean-Claude Van Damme

I was also influenced by Jhoon Rhee. He is a Tae Kwon Do instructor. I had bought some of his books and videos. Then when Jean-Claude Van Damme arrived on the scene, well what can I say, the fight scenes were awesome.

4

Chapter 4

My Karate Training Begins

Tang Soo Do

It was in 1982, I was living in Tulsa, OK. I traveled to Broken Arrow, a suburb of Tulsa, a couple days a week to attend Tang Soo Do classes. I had found out that Chuck Norris was a Black Belt in Tang Soo Do, he learned it while in Korea, while serving in the Air Force.

My brother John and I took classes at that school for about 6 months. We both got bored with the training there. I think because of not being that organized. We both received our Orange Belt while training there.

Tae Kwon Do

I had learned that my best friend from High School, and also who was my best man at my first Wedding, was taking Tae Kwon Do from a Korean Master. I joined the TKD classes in 1983 with a friend I had worked with at the pipeline company.

9

I dropped out of TKD after I got my yellow belt, because I didn't like the teaching style. Didn't know what or why we were learning certain moves and forms. They threw the White Belts in to spar with Red and Black Belts. Maybe I didn't stay long enough to get that far in the training.

5

Chapter 5

Taking A Break From Training

At this time in my life, my second daughter was born in 1983. I decided to take a break from training and concentrate on working and raising my family. We decided to move to Maine, my wife at that time was from Maine.

So, I transferred with the Post Office to Maine in 1987. By the time we got settled and bought our first house, it was just work, work, work. I was gaining weight, too many donuts, not enough working out I guess. I didn't have any ambition for training during this time.

It wasn't until many years later, after the Karate Kid movies had been around for a while. I watched them with my daughters and got the desire for more training.

But one problem, I didn't want to learn just for myself. My daughters were getting older, so I wanted them to learn also. I checked around town for martial arts schools, it was slim pickings. It was way too expensive for 3 of us at that time, only so much money to go around.

6

Chapter 6

My Desire For Something New

The year was 1994, I was 35 years old. I had the desire to get back into shape, some kind of shape, and lose my gut, that I had gained from all the donuts I had been eating. I had done weight training when I was in my early twenties, now I wanted to do something new.

I bought a Black Belt Magazine at the store, while shopping for goods. After I got home, I started looking and reading the articles in that magazine. I came upon an ad in that Black Belt Magazine, it was a full page ad, and a picture of two men posing in a stance. Those 2 men were the founders of "The Karate Connection", Chuck Sullivan and Vic LeRoux.

In their ad, they were offering a Kenpo Karate Home Study Course, and a free IKCA preview video tape. They were asking only for me to pay shipping & handling, at that time it was around $5. I immediately ordered that preview tape. I was asking myself, if I could really learn

Kenpo Karate by video training?

I finally received that tape in the mail, and watched it, I think it was around 25 minutes long. Here is what was on that tape. They came out and introduced themselves, explained what their martial arts experiences were.

Then they showed a segment from each Colored Belt Video. They explained there was a training tape for each belt level: Yellow, Orange, Purple, Blue, Green, Brown, and Black Belt. They also explained how you could learn, practice, and even test for that first level by video recording a test, then mailing it to them.

The test for each level was shown at the end of each video, there was also a test script for the person reading the test, while you are performing the test. The only catch was, you would have to videotape yourself performing the test, and mail it in to them to evaluate. I said okay, that is doable, even though I didn't have a camcorder.

7

Chapter 7

My Chinese Kenpo Karate Training Begins

Instead of ordering one belt level tape at a time, I ordered all 7 videos because of a discount for the bundle. I started watching and practicing the movements I was being taught, they even showed the movements from front, right side, left side, and rear views. I thought that was brilliant, you could really see what was going on here.

My First Test Orange Belt

About 1 month after I had started watching the Orange Belt tape, I wanted to take the test. But I had one problem, I didn't own a camcorder. So, I borrowed one from my father-in-law, recorded my test and mailed it to their Headquarters in California.

It was about 2 weeks later, I received my test tape back in the mail. What they had done after watching my test, they had recorded their response to my test at the end of my test tape. The person evaluating my test was Vic LeRoux, Senior Instructor at that time. He welcomed me to the

IKCA and started to explain the things I was doing right, then things I was doing wrong, and then physically showed me how to correct those mistakes.

I thought that was great, I was being taught one on one. Later he explained that by doing individual testing, you get a personal relationship with the Instructor. He said if it was a group class testing, many mistakes would be missed in a group. I passed the test on condition that I would correct those mistakes, and he could tell on the next test if I had corrected or not. I received my Orange Belt and promotion certificate in Chinese Kenpo. I then took his advice and corrected my mistakes.

He then explained how the testing through the belt levels worked. He would be evaluating my tests up through to Brown Belt. Chuck Sullivan, the Head Instructor at the IKCA, would be evaluating the Black Belt tests and testing for degrees within Black Belt.

That first test was all about the basic individual moves, no need to partner up yet. The next test would require a dummy partner, someone who would try to punch, kick, or put you in a bear hug. This was required after all, this is Karate training. My training partner was my nephew Gary Emerson, he was my dummy on my Purple Belt test.

My Second Test Purple Belt

Basically, the second test would require me to perform the self defense techniques taught from the Orange level on my partner. I would also perform the Short Form taught in the first tape, along with the Purple Belt techniques from different angles that I had just learned from the second tape. I had to perform the kicking drill, which was taught on the Purple Belt tape.

I got my test back for Purple Belt. Vic explained that my dummy partner was too tall for me. Gary was around 6' 2", I'm only 5' 7" tall. Vic said on my next test I would have to find another dummy partner, someone around my height. I did pass the test and was promoted to Purple Belt.

In the meantime, I was reading the quarterly IKCA newsletter that they would send to members. One of the articles was about a 3rd Degree Black belt from another Karate system, who tested for his Chinese Kenpo Orange Belt, he failed the test.

As I read the rest of the article, the guy who had just failed his Orange Belt test said that these guys (the IKCA) are serious. This was reassuring for me, I knew I had made a good decision to pursue this further. As a side note, the guy who failed that test is now a IKCA Chinese Kenpo Certified Black Belt Instructor.

My Third Test Blue Belt

So here I was, having to find another dummy partner for my next Blue Belt Test. I would still train with Gary, but still needed to test with someone shorter. My family and I went on vacation to visit my Wife's Brother and his family in Virginia.

While I was there, I tried to talk my Brother-in-law into being my dummy for my test. He wasn't interested, I didn't blame him, I didn't have any mats with me. There were some take downs on the test, my dummy partner would have to know how to fall properly.

After visiting my Brother-in-law in Virginia, we headed west to Oklahoma to visit my family there. While in Oklahoma, my Brother John agreed to be my dummy for the Blue Belt test. He was more my size, and we had previously studied Tang Soo Do together, he knew how to fall correctly. I still didn't have any mats, my Brother would be falling on a hardwood floor. He padded up with shin and knee pads, and we recorded the test.

By now, my family and I were back in Maine. I got my Blue Belt test back from IKCA Headquarters, I had passed and was promoted to Blue Belt with the IKCA. At this time, I just want to mention that I was really impressed with the IKCA training so far. I had learned more in 4 months than I had learned from attending actual school classes previously. I was sold, I would do whatever it took to continue with the IKCA.

My Fourth Test Green Belt

Here I was at this point, my next test was going to require that I find another dummy partner. I thought to myself, I'll try and find a local karate event to attend. I did find one, and attended as a viewer in the audience.

While I was watching the event, I noticed something. There was a guy wearing a Gi with the Karate Connection Patch on it. He looked to be very good at sparring and performing the Blue Belt form. After the event, I went up and introduced myself, he knew who I was. His name is Charlie Page.

The reason Charlie knew who I was from the IKCA newsletters, they would post names and locations of members that received promotions. He was also a Blue Belt with the IKCA, I had just found my new training partner. We started working toward the Green Belt test.

I would travel about 45 minutes one way, he lived in another town. He had access to a gym in his local school, this is where we would train together over the next year and a half. Charlie and I both tested and passed the Green Belt test. Now we were now both IKCA Green Belts.

My Fifth Test Brown Belt

Charlie and I continued on our path to Brown Belt over the next few months. The tests were getting longer and harder now, each belt level required you to learn and perform new techniques for that belt level. We both tested for Brown Belt and we both passed and were promoted.

We both trained hard at the Brown Belt level. At this point, I had been training in Chinese Kenpo for a little over 1 year. I trained at the Brown Belt level for about 10 or 11 months.

8

Chapter 8

Meeting My Instructors In Person

It was now about 9 or 10 months since my promotion to Brown Belt. There was an IKCA Seminar coming up in New York State in 1996, I signed up to be there. I felt I needed to be there, it just didn't feel right to test for my Black Belt yet. I didn't think I was good enough to test for the Black Belt. I was having second thoughts about ever testing for Black Belt.

So, I packed up my family and we headed from Maine to New York for the Seminar, which was held for 2 days on a weekend. We settled in the Motel and got something to eat. I was really excited to meet my Instructors in person, for the first time.

When I got to the Kenpo School, where the Seminar was held, I walked inside. There was Chuck Sullivan and Vic LeRoux in the flesh. Vic gave me a hug, and introduced me to Chuck. Remember, Vic had brought me up to Brown Belt, so this was the first time Chuck had seen me. Then Chuck gave me a hug too and said welcome to the IKCA, it was like we were all family.

I also met many other IKCA members that were there from different locations in the USA and some from Canada. There were even some Black Belts from other Karate Systems there participating in the Seminar to learn the Chinese Kenpo System.

I was also to learn that Black Belts in other systems that were there, had switched over to IKCA Kenpo System. Now that got me thinking, I am really impressed now. These people, some with multiple Black Belts in different systems were there, learning to get their Kenpo Black Belt.

On the first day of the Seminar, they broke us up into two groups, beginners and advanced. Green Belt and above went into the advanced group, Blue Belt and lower ranks including the Black Belts that weren't in the system, went to the beginner group. Chuck taught the beginner class, and Vic taught the advanced group.

The first thing that Vic did with the advanced group, the group I was in, was going over the basic moves. All the stances, stance changes, maneuvers, blocks, punches, kicks, etc. He wanted to clear up any bad habits if we had any with the basics.

Next, he went over most of the techniques up to Brown Belt, he watched us like a hawk, correcting everyone's bad habits on the spot. This was eye opening, these guys were serious about their Kenpo, they wanted their students to come away from that seminar with a clear understanding of their Chinese Kenpo.

The second day of the seminar, we ran through some of the unique drills that the IKCA practice. One drill is called running the line. The first person in the line turns around and faces the line of people, then the person facing the one in front attacks with a punch or back fist. The person defending, the one that is facing the line, performs the proper Kenpo technique for that attack.

Then after defending attacks from all the people in the line, they would move to the end of the line. The next person in front would turn and repeat the same. We would run through that drill a few times. I could see I was on par with everyone else, some of the new Black Belts would freeze, not remembering the proper technique. It's something you have to practice, in order to get good at it.

Another variation of the line drill we did was the person in the front of the line would have his or her back turned and the next person in line would put on a grab, or some hold like a bear hug, headlock, rear choke, or arm or shoulder grab from behind.

The person defending would have to perform the appropriate Kenpo technique to escape. Then after everyone in line did the grab, the person in front would move to the end of the line, and the next person in front would step forward and defend against the grab or hold.

Then came the semi-circle drill. This drill went like this. The person defending would have 5 attackers spread out at angles. So, if you were the person defending, there was one attacker directly in front of you, then two more attackers on the right flank, and two more attackers on the left flank.

The Instructor would stand behind you and point to one of the attackers, his signal to attack, so you never knew who would be attacking. You would have to move and defend with the proper technique from that angle of attack. Chuck would call this drill the circle of humiliation, because this one really takes a lot of practice.

After the seminar was over, Vic asked when he would see my Black Belt test? I told him I didn't think I was ready, he said I was ready. He said he would be watching that test with Chuck. Chuck is the one who approves all Black Belts, he is the Head Instructor with the IKCA.

9

Chapter 9

My Black Belt Test

It was about a month after I had attended the seminar in New York State. I had strained my calf muscle while at that seminar, and wanted it to heal before I submitted my test. I had contacted Charlie and we scheduled the day of the test. Since there were techniques against 2 attackers on the test, he got his brother to help us out on the test.

I got the test back from the IKCA, I had passed and was promoted to 1st Degree Black Belt. One thing that Chuck told me on that test was that I should start teaching if I wanted to. He said the greatest teacher in the world was teaching. I had no idea what he was talking about, until later...

...

10

Chapter 10

My Instructor Certification

This was in 1996, I had achieved the rank of Black Belt in 26 months of training with the IKCA. I started looking for people that might want to learn Chinese Kenpo. The next goal was to become a IKCA Certified Instructor. To accomplish this, I would have to bring someone up through the system all the way to Black Belt.

I don't really remember how I found my first certification student, or if he found me. His name is Tim Stewart, and he was my certification student up to Brown Belt. Here is the way it went. I would teach Tim from the beginning, record his test, and send it in to the IKCA.

Vic would evaluate the test, and show me on the video response, exactly what needed to be corrected and why. It went this way all the way up through the Belt levels. Tim had injured his neck, and had to cease training. This was in 2001.

So here I was so close to becoming a IKCA Certified Instructor. I was almost ready to give it up. I started running an ad in the weekly local paper for Kenpo Karate Classes. I was contacted by Keith Blanchard, but he wouldn't be ready to start training till months later. He did eventually get back to me, and we started his training. He had no prior experience, he told me that he never even kicked a soccer ball.

At this point, I could teach, test, and promote anyone up to and including Brown Belt without IKCA approval. So, that's what I did. Keith and I spent 21 months together, twice a week training. He was the only student, so I could spend one on one time with him.

He also practiced in his free time at home, he progressed faster than expected. We recorded his Black Belt test and mailed it into the IKCA. He was now a IKCA Black Belt, and I was a IKCA Certified Instructor. I was a 3rd Degree Black Belt at this time in 2004.

Keith and I started teaching more people, he would teach someone in his basement. I would teach a small group in my basement. I remember Chuck had told me, the greatest teacher is teaching, and he was absolutely right about that. He even acknowledges he has learned from his students.

11

Chapter 11

Our Trip To California

There was an event scheduled in Long Beach, California. This was in 2005, it was hosted by the IKCA. It was called the West Coast Kenpo Confederation. Keith and I jumped on a plane and flew to California for the event. We knew that Kenpo practitioners from around the world would be there. Keith had never met the Grand Masters Chuck and Vic in person, this was his chance to meet and train with them.

L to R, David Little, GM Chuck Sullivan 2005

We arrived at LAX, it was my first time there, Keith was familiar with the area. He was stationed in San Diego when he was in the Navy. We rented a car, and Keith drove us to Vic's house. It was great, Vic showed us the 57 Nomad he was rebuilding. Then he took us to his favorite Thai restaurant, and we had some lunch with some other IKCA members with us.

L to R, David Little and Keith Blanchard at GM Vic's house 2005

We were in California for 4 days, training with other Kenpo Instructors from around the world. They were from Australia, Denmark, Sweden, Canada, and many more I'm sure. I didn't get the chance to meet everyone. The event was set up as different classes, you could pick and choose what class you wanted to attend.

L to R, GM Vic LeRoux, Keith Blanchard, GM Chuck Sullivan 2005

Brenda King and GM Vic LeRoux teaching JKD trapping 2005

There were Instructors there from all the Kenpo Schools, American Kenpo, BKF Kenpo, IKCA Kenpo, and many more. We did get the opportunity to meet and train with many old time Kenpo Greats like, the Grandmasters of the BKF (Black Karate Federation), Steve Muhammed and Donnie Williams.

Grandmasters of the BKF, Steve Muhammed seated, Donnie Williams standing 2005

12

Conclusion

I would test every three years for my next degree, my last test was 2009. I was promoted to 6th Degree Black Belt in April 2009. This was the last time I would test. I continued to teach until 2017. I don't want to say I'm retired, so I'll just say I'm taking a break from teaching.

I want to thank you for reading this book. I hope it will inspire some of you to never quit striving for that goal you have in the back of your mind. Whatever martial art you train in, give it your best shot. Maybe you will write about your own journey, whatever that might be.

If you enjoyed this book, I would appreciate it if you would leave a favorable review for the book on Amazon!